THE POCKET BOOK OF
NATIVE AMERICAN WISDOM

A collection of inspiring reflections and profound spiritual knowledge

ARCTURUS

ARCTURUS

This edition published in 2022 by Arcturus Publishing Limited
26/27 Bickels Yard, 151–153 Bermondsey Street,
London SE1 3HA

ISBN: 978-1-78428-621-7
AD005613US

Printed in China

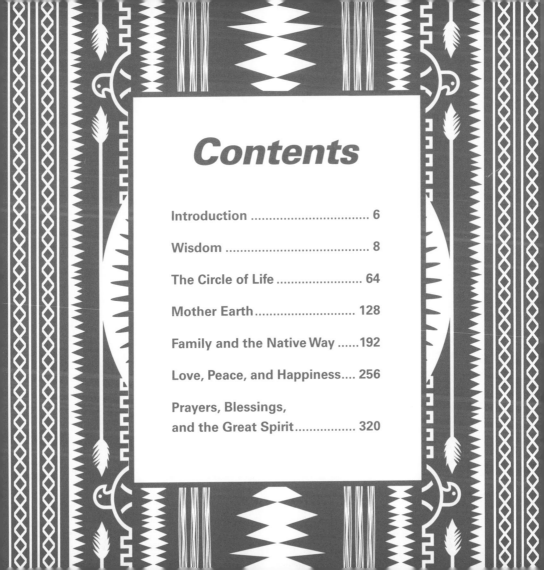

Contents

The history of the Native American people is one of turbulence and upheaval. Their encounters with European settlers since the late 15th century have become the stuff of legend, with characters such as Pocahontas, Sitting Bull, Crazy Horse, and Geronimo being immortalized in literature and cinema.

History, said Winston Churchill, is written by the victors. In the case of the Native Americans, it was written by the white settlers because writing was their method of recording both fact and fiction, while the Native Americans passed their version of events from generation to generation via the oral tradition. As a result, much of the account of the Native Americans' plight in the US and

Canada has portrayed them as savages.

This warped picture was well summed up by the 18th-century Shawnee chief Cheeseekau when he said, "When a white army battles Indians and wins, it is called a great victory, but if they lose it is called a massacre."

In recent years a more accurate portrait of the Native American has emerged: noble, brave, disciplined, selfless, honorable, resourceful, peaceful, spiritual, and deeply philosophical.

These traits shine out from this collection of quotes, gathered over the centuries as the Native Americans sought to preserve their harmonious way of life against all the odds.

Wisdom

Seek wisdom, not knowledge. Knowledge is of the past, Wisdom is of the future.

Lumbee proverb

Friend do it this way—that is, whatever you do in life,
do the very best you can with both your heart and mind.
And if you do it that way, the Power Of The Universe
will come to your assistance, if your heart and mind are in Unity.
When one sits in the Hoop Of The People, one must be responsible because
All of Creation is related.
And the hurt of one is the hurt of all.
And the honor of one is the honor of all.
And whatever we do affects everything in the Universe.
If you do it that way—that is, if you truly join your heart and mind as One—
whatever you ask for, that's the way it's going to be.

Pte Ska Win (White Buffalo Calf Woman), Lakota
Sioux

11

You have noticed that everything an Indian does is in a circle, and that is because the Power of the World always works in circles, and everything tries to be round.

Black Elk, Oglala Lakota Sioux

Honor the sacred.
Honor the Earth, our Mother.
Honor the Elders.
Honor all with whom we share the Earth:
Four-leggeds, two-leggeds, winged ones,
Swimmers, crawlers, plant and rock people.
Walk in balance and beauty.

Unknown elder

Silence has so much meaning.

Yukon proverb

Silence is the mother of truth, for the silent man is ever to be trusted, while the man ever ready with speech was never taken seriously.

Chief Luther Standing Bear,
Oglala Lakota Sioux

15

Thought comes before speech.

Chief Luther Standing Bear,
Oglala Lakota Sioux

A very great vision is needed and the man who has it must follow it as the eagle seeks the deepest blue of the sky.

Tasunke Witko (Crazy Horse),
Oglala Lakota Sioux

Never pass up a chance to keep your mouth shut.

Will Rogers, Cherokee

A good soldier is a poor scout.

Cheyenne proverb

A starving man will eat with the wolf.

Oklahoma proverb

Honor does the right thing, even when no one is looking.

Siyotanka (John Two-Hawks),
Oglala Lakota Sioux

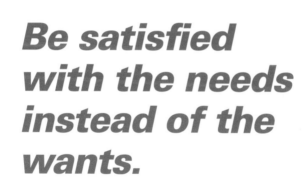

Be satisfied with the needs instead of the wants.

Teton Sioux proverb

*It is better
to have less
thunder in the
mouth and
more lightning
in the hand.*

Apache proverb

Silence is the absolute poise or balance of body, mind, and spirit.

Ohiyesa (Dr Charles Alexander Eastman), Santee Dakota Sioux

Even a small mouse has anger.

Unattributed proverb

To speak wisely, one must listen humbly.

Siyotanka (John Two-Hawks), Oglala Lakota Sioux

After dark all cats are leopards.

Zuni proverb

Beware of the man who does not talk, and the dog that does not bark.

Cheyenne proverb

Do not allow anger to poison you.

Hopi proverb

Friendship
between
two persons
depends upon
the patience
of one.

Unattributed proverb

It is less of a problem
to be poor, than to be
dishonest.

Anishinabe proverb

Listening to a liar is like drinking warm water.

Unattributed proverb

Most of us do not look as handsome to others as we do to ourselves.

Assiniboine proverb

A man must make his own arrows.

Winnebago proverb

The man who preserves
his selfhood ever calm and
unshaken by the storms of
existence—not a leaf, as it
were, astir on the tree, not a
ripple upon the surface of the
shining pool—his, in the mind
of the unlettered sage, is the
ideal attitude and conduct of
life... Silence is the cornerstone
of character.

Ohiyesa (Dr Charles Alexander Eastman),
Santee Dakota Sioux

The coward shoots with shut eyes.

Otoe proverb

The moon is not shamed by the barking of dogs.

Southwest proverb

The rain falls on the just and the unjust.

Hopi proverb

The way of the troublemaker is thorny.

Umpqua proverb

The weakness of the enemy makes our strength.

Cherokee proverb

Those that lie
down with dogs,
get up with fleas.

Blackfoot proverb

You can't wake a person who is pretending to be asleep.

Navajo proverb

A danger foreseen is half-avoided.

Cheyenne proverb

Don't believe the dark whisperings that invite you to walk backward. At any time in your life, you have the power to turn forward.

From The Seven Paths: Changing One's Way of Walking in the World, *Anasazi Foundation*

Each morning offers lessons in light. For the morning light teaches the most basic of truths: Light chases away darkness.

Anasazi Foundation

There are many
good moccasin
tracks along the trail
of a straight arrow.

Sioux proverb

For my part, I am of the opinion that so far as we have reason, we have the right to use it in determining what is right or wrong, and we should pursue that path we believe to be right.

Chief Black Hawk, Sauk

Touch not the poisonous firewater that makes wise ones turn to fools and robs their spirit of its vision.

Chief Tecumseh, Shawnee

All dreams spin out from the same web.

Hopi proverb

Do not only point out the way, but lead the way.

Sioux proverb

We have men among us, like the whites, who pretend to know the right path, but will not consent to show it without pay! I have no faith in their paths, but believe that every man must make his own path!

Chief Black Hawk, Sauk

Western civilization, unfortunately, does not link knowledge and morality but rather, it connects knowledge and power and makes them equivalent.

Vine Deloria Jr., Oglala Lakota Sioux

Everyone who is successful must have dreamed of something.

Maricopa proverb

Each person is his own judge.

Shawnee proverb

When you begin a great work you can't expect to finish it all at once; therefore do you and your brothers press on, and let nothing discourage you till you have entirely finished what you have begun.

Teedyuscung, King of the Delawares

He who is present at a wrongdoing and does not lift a hand to prevent it is as guilty as the wrongdoers.

Unattributed proverb

It is easy to be brave from a distance.

Omaha proverb

Make my enemy brave and strong, so that if defeated, I will not be ashamed.

Plains proverb

No one else can represent your conscience.

Anishinabe proverb

Speak truth in humility to all people. Only then can you be a true man.

Sioux proverb

Strive to be a person who is never absent from an important act.

Osage proverb

Those who have one foot in the canoe and one foot in the boat are going to fall into the river.

Tuscarora proverb

If we wonder often, the gift of knowledge will come.

Arapaho proverb

Knowledge that is
not used is abused.

Cree proverb

Listen, or your
tongue will
make you deaf.

Unattributed proverb

Tell me and I'll forget. Show me and I may not remember. Involve me and I'll understand.

Unattributed proverb

The one who tells the stories rules the world.

Hopi proverb

Wisdom comes only when you stop looking for it and start living the life the Creator intended for you.

Hopi proverb

We do not want schools —they will teach us to have churches. We do not want churches—they will teach us to quarrel about God. We do not want to learn that.

Heinmot Tooyalaket (Chief Joseph), Nez Percé

The Great Spirit raised both the white man and the Indian. I think he raised the Indian first.

Chief Red Cloud, Oglala Lakota Sioux

When you know who you are, when your mission is clear and you burn with the inner fire of unbreakable will, no cold can touch your heart, no deluge can dampen your purpose. You know that you are alive.

Chief Seattle, Suqwamish and Duwamish

You have to look deeper, way below the anger, the hurt, the hate, the jealousy, the self-pity, way down deeper where the dreams lie, son. Find your dream. It's the pursuit of the dream that heals you.

Father of Olympic gold medalist Billy Mills,
Oglala Lakota Sioux

In my youth I respected the world and life, I needed not anything but peace of heart;
And yet I changed despite myself and believed in Iktumi's lies.
He seemed to know all the truth, he promised to make me happy.
He made me ask Wakan Tanka for wealth, that I might have power;
I was given poverty, that I might find my inner strength.
I asked for fame, so others would know me;
I was given obscurity, that I might know myself.

Olympic gold medalist Billy Mills, Oglala Lakota Sioux (In Lakota folklore, Iktumi is a trickster spirit in spider form.)

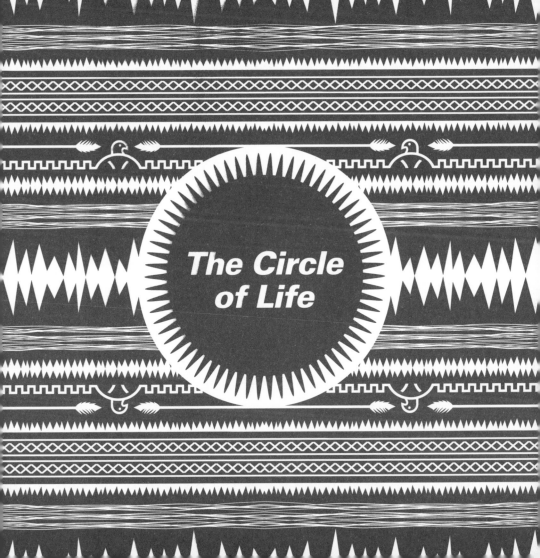

The Circle of Life

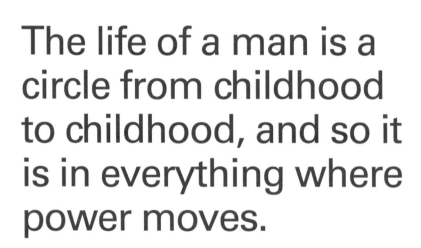

The life of a man is a circle from childhood to childhood, and so it is in everything where power moves.

Black Elk, Oglala Lakota Sioux

Old age is not as honorable as death, but most people want it.

Crow proverb

We are like birds with a broken wing. My heart is cold within me. My eyes are growing dim—I am old.

Chief Plenty Coups, Crow

Often in summer I rise at daybreak and steal out to the cornfields, and as I hoe the corn I sing to it, as we did when I was young.
No one cares for our corn songs now.

Waheenee-Wea (Buffalo Bird Woman), Hidatsa Sioux (from Waheenee: An Indian Girl's Story, *by Gilbert L. Wilson)*

What! Would you wish that there should be no dried trees in the woods and no dead branches on a tree that is growing old?

A 70-year-old Huron

Cherish youth, but trust old age.

Pueblo proverb

Don't let yesterday use up too much of today.

Cherokee proverb

**Make me always
ready to come to you
With clean hands
and straight eyes.
So when life fades,
as the fading sunset,
My Spirit may come
to you without
shame.**

*Great Spirit Prayer, translated by
Chief Yellow Lark, Lakota Sioux*

Grown men can learn from very little children, for the hearts of the little children are pure. Therefore, the Great Spirit may show to them many things which older people miss.

Black Elk, Oglala Lakota Sioux

I cannot tell you the dreamy, Indian story of your imagination, simply because I am not imaginary, and my story is no dream.

Siyotanka (John Two-Hawks),
Oglala Lakota Sioux

Our young people, raised under old rules of courtesy, never indulged in the present habit of talking incessantly and all at the same time. To do so would have been not only impolite but foolish; for poise, so much admired as a social grace, could not be accompanied by restlessness.

Chief Luther Standing Bear,
Oglala Lakota Sioux

Civilization has been thrust upon me since the days of the reservations, and it has not added one whit to my sense of justice, to my reverence for the rights of life, to my love for truth, honesty, and generosity, or to my faith in Wakan Tanka, God of the Lakotas.

Chief Luther Standing Bear, Oglala Lakota Sioux

Sometimes in the evening I sit, looking out on the big Missouri. The sun sets, and dusk steals over the water. In the shadows I seem again to see our Indian village, with smoke curling upward from the earth lodges, and in the river's roar I hear the yells of the warriors, and the laughter of little children of old.
It is but an old woman's dream.

Waheenee-Wea (Buffalo Bird Woman), Hidatsa Sioux (from Waheenee: An Indian Girl's Story, *by Gilbert L. Wilson)*

Because we are old, it may be thought that the memory of things may be lost with us, who have not, like you, the art of preserving it by committing all transactions to writing. We nevertheless have methods of transmitting from father to son an account of all these things. You will find the remembrance of them is faithfully preserved, and our succeeding generations are made acquainted with what has passed, that it may not be forgot as long as the earth remains.

*Chief Kanickhungo, Seneca Iroquois
(at treaty negotiations with Six Nations)*

When the Micmac people used to have council, the old men would speak and tell the young men what to do—and the young men would listen and do what the old men told them to do. The white men have changed that too: Now the young men speak, and the old men listen. I believe the Micmac council was far better.

Chief Peter Paul Toney Babey, Micmac

We will be known
forever by the
tracks we leave.

Dakota proverb

Eventually one gets to the Medicine Wheel to fulfill one's life.

Old Mouse, Arikara (The Medicine Wheel is a place of worship and a National Historic Site, located high in the Big Horn Mountains. Believed to have been constructed some time between AD1200 and 1700, it comprises hundreds of limestone rocks placed in the shape of a spoked wheel.)

You must live
your life from
beginning to end:
No one else can
do it for you.

Hopi proverb

A brave man dies but once, a coward many times.

Unattributed proverb

All who have died are equal.

Comanche proverb

At the end of our lives, when our bodies are about to be laid in Mother Earth, we will know for ourselves whether we are a Two-Legged being full of light or a Two-Legged being full of darkness.

From The Seven Paths: Changing One's Way of Walking in the World, *Anasazi Foundation*

But why should I mourn the untimely fate of my people? Your time of decay may be distant, but it will surely come, for even the white man, whose God walked and talked with him as friend with friend, cannot be exempt from the common destiny. We may be brothers, after all. We will see...

Chief Seattle, Suqwamish and Duwamish

Do not grieve. Misfortunes will happen to the wisest and best of men. Death will come, always out of season. It is the command of the Great Spirit, and all nations and people must obey. What is past and what cannot be prevented should not be grieved for... Misfortunes do not flourish particularly in our lives— they grow everywhere.

Chief Big Elk, Omaha

And when the last red man shall have perished, and the memory of my tribe shall have become a myth among the white men, these shores will swarm with the invisible dead of my tribe; and when our children's children think themselves alone in the field, the store, the shop, upon the highway, or in the silence of the pathless woods, they will not be alone.

Chief Seattle, Suqwamish and Duwamish

Grandfather says that when your friends die you must not cry. You must not hurt anybody or do harm to anyone. You must not fight. Do right always. It will give you satisfaction in life.

Wovoka (Jack Wilson), Paiute

I want to have time to look for my children and see how many I can find. Maybe I shall find them among the dead.
Hear me, my chiefs. I am tired. My heart is sick and sad. From where the sun now stands, I will fight no more forever.

Heinmot Tooyalaket (Chief Joseph), Nez Percé

I know that robes, leggings, moccasins, bear claws, and so on are of little value to you, but we wish you have them and to preserve them in some conspicuous part of your lodge, so that when we are gone and the sod turned over our bones, if our children should visit this place, as we do now, they may see and recognize with pleasure the things of their fathers, and reflect on the times that are past.

Chief Sharitarish, Grand Pawnee

I was born upon a
prairie where the wind
blew free and there
was nothing to break
the light of the sun. I
was born where there
were no enclosures and
where everything drew
a free breath.
I want to die there, and
not within walls.

Chief Ten Bears, Yamparika Comanche

I'll be coming back as lightning, so if you live longer than me, and you hear that lightning has struck the White House, you'll know who did it!

Wanbli Ohitika (Russell Means),
Oglala Lakota Sioux

Life is not separate from death. It only looks that way.

Blackfoot proverb

If my warriors are to fight they are too few; if they are to die they are too many.

Hendrick Theyanoguin, Mohawk

Live your life that the fear of death can never enter your heart.

Chief Tecumseh, Shawnee

Remember:
If the Creator
put it there, it
is in the right
place. The soul
would have no
rainbow if the
eyes had no
tears.

Unknown Indian Chief

Take only memories, leave nothing but footprints.

Unattributed proverb

There are but two ways for us. One leads to hunger and death, the other leads to where the poor white man lives. Beyond is the happy hunting ground where the white man cannot go.

Many Horses, Oglala Lakota Sioux

There is no death, only
a change of worlds.

Chief Seattle, Suqwamish and Duwamish

There is nothing as eloquent as a rattlesnake's tail.

Navajo proverb

They are not dead
who live in the hearts
they leave behind.

Tuscarora proverb

We are made from Mother Earth and we go back to Mother Earth.

Shenandoah proverb

We live, we die, and like the grass and trees, renew ourselves from the soft earth of the grave. Stones crumble and decay, faiths grow old and they are forgotten, but new beliefs are born. The faith of the villages is dust now... but it will grow again... like the trees.

Heinmot Tooyalaket (Chief Joseph), Nez Percé

What is life? It is the flash of a firefly in the night. It is the breath of a buffalo in the wintertime. It is the little shadow which runs across the grass and loses itself in the sunset.

Chief Crowfoot, Siksika

When you die, you will be spoken of as those in the sky, like the stars.

Yurok proverb

When you were born, you cried and the world rejoiced. Live your life so that when you die, the world cries and you rejoice.

Cherokee proverb

When your time comes to die, be not like those whose hearts are filled with fear of death, so that when their time comes they weep and pray for a little more time to live their lives over again in a different way. Sing your death song, and die like a hero going home.

Chief Tecumseh, Shawnee

What is past and cannot be prevented should not be grieved for.

Pawnee proverb

Many have fallen with the bottle in their hand.

Lakota Sioux proverb

Good words do not last long unless they amount to something. Words do not pay for my dead people. They do not pay for my country, now overrun by white men. They do not protect my father's grave. They do not pay for all my horses and cattle. Good words will not give back my children. Good words will not make good the promise of your War Chief. Good words will not give my people good health and stop them from dying. Good words will not get my people a home where they can live in peace and take care of themselves. I am tired of talk that comes to nothing.

Heinmot Tooyalaket (Chief Joseph), Nez Percé, on a visit to Washington, D.C., 1879

Through drinking, seven score of our people have been killed. The cask must be sealed, it must be made fast; it must not leak by day or night, in the light or in the dark.

Okanicon, Delaware

Don't be afraid to cry. It will free your mind of sorrowful thoughts.

Hopi proverb

I was warmed by the sun, rocked by the winds, and sheltered by the trees, as other Indian babes. I can go everywhere with a good feeling.

Geronimo, Apache

Earth teach me stillness as the grasses are stilled with light.

Earth teach me suffering as old stones suffer with memory.

Earth teach me humility as blossoms are humble with beginning.

Earth teach me caring as the mother who secures her young.

Earth teach me courage as the tree which stands alone.

Earth teach me limitation as the ant which crawls on the ground.

Earth teach me freedom as the eagle which soars in the sky.

Earth teach me resignation as the leaves which die in the fall.

Earth teach me regeneration as the seed which rises in the spring.

Earth teach me to forget myself as melted snow forgets its life.

Earth teach me to remember kindness as dry fields weep in the rain.

Chief Yellow Lark, Lakota

I asked for power, that I might achieve;
I was given weakness, that I might
learn to obey.
I asked for health, that I might lead a
long life;
I was given infirmity, that I might
appreciate each minute.
I asked Mother Earth for strength, that
I might have my way;
I was given weakness, that I might
feel the need for Her.
I asked to live happily, that I might
enjoy life;
I was given life, that I might live
happily.
I received nothing I asked for, yet all
my wishes came true.

Olympic gold medalist Billy Mills,
Oglala Lakota Sioux

Love your life, perfect your life, beautify all things in your life.
Seek to make your life long and of service to your people.
Prepare a noble death song for the day when you go over the great divide.

Chief Tecumseh, Shawnee

Man's law changes with his understanding of man. Only the laws of the spirit remain always the same.

Crow proverb

The path to glory is rough, and many gloomy hours obscure it. May the Great Spirit shed light on your path, so that you may never experience the humility that the power of the American government has reduced me to. This is the wish of a man who, in his native forests, was once as proud and bold as yourself.

Chief Black Hawk, Sauk

That is why the old Indian still sits upon the earth instead of propping himself up and away from its life-giving forces. For him, to sit or lie upon the ground is to be able to think more deeply and to feel more keenly. He can see more clearly into the mysteries of life and come closer in kinship to other lives about him.

Chief Luther Standing Bear, Oglala Lakota Sioux

In sharing, in loving all and everything, one people naturally found a due portion of the thing they sought, while, in fearing, the other found the need of conquest. For one man the world was full of beauty, for the other it was a place of sin and ugliness to be endured until he went to another world, there to become a creature of wings, half-man and half-bird.

Chief Luther Standing Bear, Oglala Lakota Sioux

Guard your tongue in youth, and in age you may mature a thought that will be of service to your people.

Susquehannock proverb

In age, talk;
in childhood,
tears.

Hopi proverb

Hold on to what is good even if it is a handful of earth.
Hold on to what you believe even if it is a tree which stands by itself.
Hold on to what you must do even if it is a long way from here.
Hold on to life even when it is easier letting go.
Hold on to my hand even when I have gone away from you.

Pueblo blessing

Our old women
gods, we ask you!
Our old women
gods, we ask you!
Then give us long
life together,
May we live until our
frosted hair is white;
May we live till then.
This life that now
we know!

Tewa proverb

May the sun bring you new
energy by day
May the moon softly
restore you by night
May the rain wash away
your worries
May the breeze blow new
strength into your being
May you walk gently
through the world and
Know its beauty all the
days of your life.

Apache blessing

You already possess everything necessary to become great.

Crow proverb

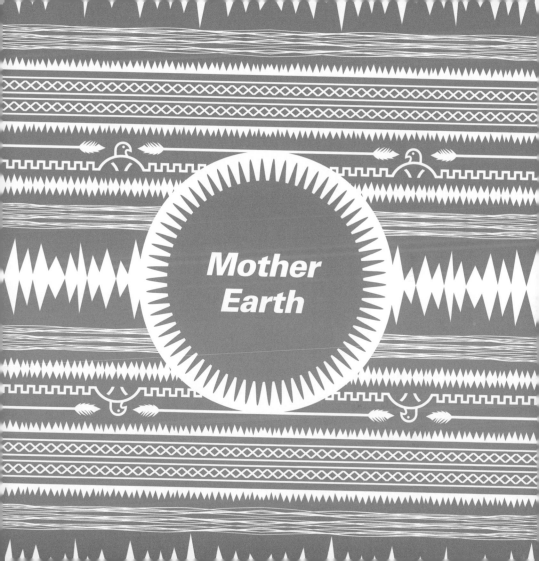

Mother Earth

The frog does not drink up the pond in which it lives.

Unattributed proverb

Nothing can be sold, except things that can be carried away.

Chief Black Hawk, Sauk

The sun comes forth and goes down again in a circle. The moon does the same and both are round. Even the seasons form a great circle in their changing and always come back again to where they were.

Black Elk, Oglala Lakota Sioux

The true Indian sets no price upon either his property or his labor.

Ohiyesa (Dr Charles Alexander Eastman), Santee Dakota Sioux

We must go beyond the arrogance of human rights. We must go beyond the ignorance of civil rights. We must step into the reality of natural rights. Because all of the natural world has a right to existence and we are only a small part of it. There can be no trade-off.

John Trudell, Santee Dakota Sioux

A good way to start thinking about nature, talk about it. Rather talk to it, talk to the rivers, to the lakes, to the winds as to our relatives.

John Fire Lame Deer, Lakota Sioux

All plants are our brothers and sisters. They talk to us and if we listen, we can hear them.

Arapaho proverb

We do not inherit the Earth from our Ancestors, we borrow it from our Children.

Popular proverb believed to have been coined by Chief Seattle, Suqwamish and Duwamish

Before eating, always take time to thank the food.

Arapaho proverb

Continue to contaminate your own bed, and you will suffocate in your own waste.

Chief Seattle, Suqwamish and Duwamish

How can the spirit of the earth like the white man? Everywhere the white man has touched it, it is sore.

Unknown Wintu woman

Could it be that the road to technology represents a rush to destruction, and that the road to spirituality represents the slower path that the traditional native people have traveled and are now seeking again? The earth is not scorched on this trail. The grass is still growing there.

William Commanda, Algonquin

Every animal knows more than you do.

Nez Percé proverb

Everything on the earth has a purpose, every disease a herb to cure it, and every person a mission. This is the Indian theory of existence.

Mourning Dove, Salish

From Wakan Tanka, the Great Spirit, there came a great unifying life force that flowed in and through all things—the flowers of the plains, blowing winds, rocks, trees, birds, animals—and was the same force that had been breathed into the first man. Thus all things were kindred, and were brought together by the same Great Mystery.

Chief Luther Standing Bear,
Oglala Lakota Sioux

I do not think the measure of a civilization is how tall its buildings of concrete are, but rather how well its people have learned to relate to their environment and fellow man.

Sun Bear, Ojibwe

I will tell you one of the things
we remember on our land. We
remember that our grandfathers
paid for it… with their lives.

John Woodenlegs, Cheyenne

In our every deliberation, we must consider the impact of our decisions on the next seven generations.

Iroquois maxim

It is thought great to be born in palaces, surrounded with wealth, but to be born in Nature's wide domain is greater still!

Kahgegagahbowh (George Copway), Ojibwe

Listen to the air. You can hear it, feel it, smell it, taste it. Woniya wakan —the holy air—which renews all by its breath. Woniya, woniya wakan —spirit, life, breath, renewal—it means all that. Woniya—we sit together, don't touch, but something is there; we feel it between us, as a presence.

John Fire Lame Deer, Lakota Sioux

Listen to the voice of nature, for it holds treasures for you.

Huron proverb

No man is as wise
as Mother Earth.
She has witnessed
every human day,
every human
struggle, every
human pain, and
every human joy.

From The Seven Paths: Changing One's Way
of Walking in the World, *Anasazi Foundation*

Man has responsibility, not power.

Tuscarora proverb

Live with the earth, not on top of it.

Siyotanka (John Two-Hawks), Oglala Lakota Sioux

Men must be born and reborn to belong. Their bodies must be formed of the dust of their forefathers' bones.

Chief Luther Standing Bear,
Oglala Lakota Sioux

Nature is not dumb. Humanity is dumb when we can't hear or when we forget how to communicate with nature. Nature is very much alive. Intelligent living beings and vibrant energies are all over the planet.

From Walk in Balance: The Path to Healthy, Happy, Harmonious Living by Sun Bear, *Ojibwe*

Niagara will be Niagara a thousand years hence. The rainbow, a wreath over her brow, shall continue as long as the sun and the flowing of the river, while the work of art, however carefully protected and preserved, shall fade and crumble into dust.

Kahgegagahbowh (George Copway), Ojibwe

No people have better use of their five senses than the children of the wilderness. We could smell as well as hear and see. We could feel and taste as well as we could see and hear. Nowhere has the memory been more fully developed than in the wild life.

Ohiyesa (Dr Charles Alexander Eastman), Santee Dakota Sioux

One does not sell the land people walk on.

Tasunke Witko (Crazy Horse),
Oglala Lakota Sioux

The mountains, I become a part of it.
The herbs, the fir tree, I become a part of it.
The morning mists, the clouds, the gathering waters, I become a part of it.
The wilderness, the dew drops, the pollen, I become a part of it.

Navajo chant

Only to the white man was nature a wilderness and only to him was the land "infested" with "wild" animals and "savage" people. To us it was tame, Earth was bountiful, and we were surrounded with the blessings of the Great Mystery.

Black Elk, Oglala Lakota Sioux

Our land is more valuable than your money.
It will last forever.
It will not even perish by the flames of fire.
As long as the sun shines and the waters flow, this land will be here to give life to men and animals.

Chief Crowfoot, Siksika

Some of our chiefs make the claim that the land belongs to us. It is not what the Great Spirit told me. He told me that the lands belong to Him, that no people owns the land; that I was not to forget to tell this to the white people when I met them in council.

Kanekuk, Kickapoo prophet

This is the Earth, healed again, growing green and blue. I want you to remember this exactly as it is, and then go and tell the people that if enough of us hold this image in their minds, we can heal the Earth and make it like it was a long time ago.

Rolling Thunder (John Pope), Cherokee

Take only what you need and leave the land as you found it.

Arapaho proverb

Someone needs to explain to me why wanting clean drinking water makes you an activist, and why proposing to destroy water with chemical warfare doesn't make a corporation a terrorist.

Winona LaDuke, Ojibwe

The beauty of the trees,
the softness of the air,
the fragrance of the grass,
speaks to me.
The summit of the mountain,
the thunder of the sky,
the rhythm of the sea,
speaks to me.
The strength of the fire,
the taste of salmon,
the trail of the sun,
and the life that never goes away,
they speak to me.
And my heart soars.

Geswanouth Slahoot (Chief Dan George), Tsleil-Waututh Salish

The Great Spirit is in all things, he is in the air we breathe. The Great Spirit is our Father, but the Earth is our Mother. She nourishes us, that which we put into the ground she returns to us.

Bedagi (Big Thunder), Wabanaki Algonquin

The Indian prefers the soft
sound of the wind darting
over the face of the pond,
the smell of the wind itself
cleansed by a midday rain,
or scented with pinyon
pine. The air is precious to
the red man, for all things
share the same breath—
the animals, the trees,
the man, the air shares
its spirit with all the life it
supports.

Chief Seattle, Suqwamish and Duwamish

The ground on which we stand is sacred ground. It is the dust and blood of our ancestors.

Chief Plenty Coups, Crow

One thing to remember is to talk to the animals. If you do, they will talk back to you. But if you don't talk to the animals, they won't talk back to you, then you won't understand, and when you don't understand you will fear, and when you fear you will destroy the animals, and if you destroy the animals, you will destroy yourself.

Geswanouth Slahoot (Chief Dan George), Tsleil-Waututh Salish

The Lakota was a true naturalist—a lover of Nature. He loved the earth and all things of the earth, and the attachment grew with age. The old people came literally to love the soil and they sat or reclined on the ground with a feeling of being close to a mothering power. Their teepees were built upon the earth and their altars were made of earth. The soul was soothing, strengthening, cleansing, and healing.

Chief Luther Standing Bear,
Oglala Lakota Sioux

The life of an Indian is like the wings of the air.
That is why you notice the hawk knows how to get his prey. The Indian is like that.
The hawk swoops down on its prey, so does the Indian.
In his lament he is like an animal. For instance, the coyote is sly, so is the Indian.
The eagle is the same.
That is why the Indian is always feathered up; he is a relative to the wings of the air.

Black Elk, Oglala Lakota Sioux

The old Indian teaching was that it is wrong to tear loose from its place on the earth anything that may be growing there. It may be cut off, but it should not be uprooted. The trees and the grass have spirits. Whatever one of such growth may be destroyed by some good Indian, his act is done in sadness and with a prayer for forgiveness.

John Woodenlegs, Cheyenne

The old Lakota was wise. He knew that a man's heart, away from nature, becomes hard. He knew that a lack of respect for growing, living things soon led to lack of respect for humans too. So he kept his children close to nature's softening influence.

Chief Luther Standing Bear, Oglala Lakota Sioux

The reality is that every time we manipulate nature's rhythms, we create unintended consequences that then require us to make still further changes.

Kizhe Naabe (Glenn Aparicio Parry, PhD), Ojibwe

The soil was soothing, strengthening, cleansing, and healing. This is why the old Indian still sits upon the earth instead of propping himself up and away from its life-giving forces. For him, to sit or lie upon the ground is to be able to think more deeply and to feel more keenly; he can see more clearly into the mysteries of life and come closer in kinship to other lives about him.

Chief Luther Standing Bear, Oglala Lakota Sioux

The time will soon be here when my grandchild will long for the cry of a loon, the flash of a salmon, the whisper of spruce needles, or the screech of an eagle. But he will not make friends with any of these creatures and when his heart aches with longing, he will curse me. Have I done all to keep the air fresh? Have I cared enough about the water? Have I left the eagle to soar in freedom? Have I done everything I could to earn my grandchild's fondness?

Geswanouth Slahoot (Chief Dan George), Tsleil-Waututh Salish

All things are connected.
Whatever befalls the
Earth befalls the children
of the Earth.

Chief Seattle, Suqwamish and Duwamish

There are many things to be shared with the Four Colors of humanity in our common destiny as one with our Mother the Earth. It is this sharing that must be considered with great care by the Elders and the medicine people who carry the Sacred Trusts, so that no harm may come to people through ignorance and misuse of these powerful forces.

1980 Resolution of the Fifth Annual Meeting of the Traditional Elders Circle

There is a power in nature that man has ignored. And the result has been heartache and pain.

From The Seven Paths: Changing One's Way of Walking in the World, *Anasazi Foundation*

There is no quiet place in the white man's cities, no place to hear the leaves of spring or the rustle of insects' wings. Perhaps it is because I am a savage and do not understand, but the clatter only seems to insult the ears.

Chief Seattle, Suqwamish and Duwamish

To touch the earth is to have harmony with nature.

Sioux proverb

When all the trees have been cut down, when all the animals have been hunted, when all the waters are polluted, when all the air is unsafe to breathe, only then will you discover you cannot eat money.

Cree proverb

Walk lightly in the spring; Mother Earth is pregnant.

Kiowa proverb

This we know. The earth does not belong to man; man belongs to the earth.

Chief Seattle, Suqwamish and Duwamish

We know that the land is everlasting, and the few goods we receive for it are soon worn out and gone.

Chief Canassatego, Onondaga

We must protect the forests for our children, grandchildren, and children yet to be born. We must protect the forests for those who can't speak for themselves such as the birds, animals, fish, and trees.

Chief Qwatsinas (Edward Moody), Nuxalk

What is man without the beasts? If all the beasts were gone, men would die from great loneliness of spirit, for whatever happens to the beasts also happens to man.

Chief Seattle, Suqwamish and Duwamish

When a man moves away from nature his heart becomes hard.

Lakota proverb

When asked by an anthropologist what the Indians called America before the white man came, an Indian said simply, "Ours."

Vine Deloria Jr., Oglala Lakota Sioux

The land is sacred. These words are at the core of your being. The land is our mother, the rivers our blood. Take our land away and we die. That is, the Indian in us dies.

Mary Brave Bird, Sicangu Lakota Sioux

When the buffalo are all slaughtered, the wild horses all tamed, the secret corners of the forest heavy with the scent of many men, and the view of the ripe hills blotted by talking wires, where is the thicket? Gone. Where is the eagle? Gone.

Chief Seattle, Suqwamish and Duwamish

When we Indians kill
meat, we eat it all up.
When we dig roots,
we make little holes.
When we build houses,
we make little holes.
When we burn grass for
grasshoppers, we don't
ruin things. We shake
down acorns and pine
nuts. We don't chop
down the trees. We only
use dead wood.

Unknown Wintu woman

When we show our respect for other living things, they respond with respect for us.

Arapaho proverb

Humankind has not woven
the web of life. We are but
one thread within it.

Chief Seattle, Suqwamish and Duwamish

Money to us is of no value, and to most of us unknown… no consideration whatever can induce us to sell the lands, on which we get sustenance for our women and children.

From a 1793 letter from the Seven Nations of Canada

No tribe has the right to sell, even to each other, much less to strangers. Sell a country! Why not sell the air, the great sea, as well as the earth? Didn't the Great Spirit make them all for the use of his children?

Chief Tecumseh, Shawnee
(in a speech to William Harrison,
Governor of the Indiana Territory, on
August 11, 1810)

Let us put our minds together and see what life we can make for our children.

Tatanka Iyotanka (Sitting Bull),
Hunkpapa Lakota Sioux

They made us many promises,
more than I can remember.
But they kept but one: they
promised to take our land…
and they took it.

Chief Red Cloud, Oglala Lakota Sioux

Family
and the
Native
Way

This we know.
All things are
connected like
the blood which
unites one family.
All things are
connected.

Chief Seattle, Suqwamish and Duwamish

We can say that we are at home everywhere, because we set up our wigwams with ease wherever we go, without asking permission from anyone.

Micmac Chief (recorded by 17th-century French missionary Chrétien Le Clercq)

Our teepees were round like the nests of birds, and these were always set in a circle, the nation's hoop, a nest of many nests, where the Great Spirit meant for us to hatch our children.

Black Elk, Oglala Lakota Sioux

Children learn from what they see. We need to set an example of truth and action.

Howard Rainer, Taos Pueblo

Children were encouraged to develop strict discipline and a high regard for sharing.
When a girl picked her first berries and dug her first roots, they were given away to an elder so she would share her future success.
When a child carried water for the home, an elder would give compliments, pretending to taste meat in water carried by a boy or berries in that of a girl.
The child was encouraged not to be lazy and to grow straight like a sapling.

Mourning Dove, Salish

During the first year a newly married couple discovers whether they can agree with each other and can be happy. If not, they part, and look for other partners. If we were to live together and disagree, we should be as foolish as the whites.

Chief Black Hawk, Sauk

I have been to the end of the earth.
I have been to the end of the water.
I have been to the end of the sky.
I have been to the end of the
mountains. I have found none that
are not my friends.

Unknown Navajo

Oh Great Spirit,
Be kind to us
Give these people
the favor
To see green trees,
Green grass, flowers,
and berries
This next spring;
So we all meet again
Oh Great Spirit,
We ask of you.

Mohawk prayer

A rocky vineyard does not need a prayer, but a pick ax.

Navajo proverb

We send our little Indian boys and girls to school, and when they come back talking English, they come back swearing. There is no swear word in the Indian languages, and I haven't yet learned to swear.

Zitkala-Sa (Gertrude S. Bonnin), Yankton Sioux

*What boy would not
be an Indian for a while
when he thinks of the
freest life in the world?*

*Ohiyesa (Dr Charles Alexander
Eastman), Santee Dakota Sioux*

It takes a
thousand
voices to tell
a single story.

Unattributed proverb

All birds, even those of the same species, are not alike, and it is the same with animals and with human beings.

Shooter, Lakota Sioux

Do not speak of evil for it creates curiosity in the hearts of the young.

Lakota Sioux proverb

The bird who
has eaten cannot
fly with the bird
that is hungry.

Omaha proverb

***There is a need
for obedience
all around us.***

Sauk maxim

Conversation was never begun at once, or in a hurried manner. No one was quick with a question, no matter how important, and no one was pressed for an answer. A pause giving time for thought was the truly courteous way of beginning and conducting a conversation.

Chief Luther Standing Bear,
Oglala Lakota Sioux

As a little child, it was instilled into me to be silent and reticent. This was one of the most important traits to form in the character of the Indian. As a hunter and warrior, it was considered absolutely necessary to him, and was thought to lay the foundations of patience and self-control.

Ohiyesa (Dr Charles Alexander Eastman),
Santee Dakota Sioux

What the people believe is true.

Anishinabe proverb

When a fox walks lame, the old rabbit jumps.

Oklahoma proverb

We went from being Indians to pagans to savages to hostiles to militants to activists to Native Americans. It's 500 years later and they still can't see us. We are still invisible.

John Trudell, Santee Dakota

I think that wherever the Great Spirit places his people, they ought to be satisfied to remain, and thankful for what He has given them, and not drive others from the country He has given them because it happens to be better than theirs!

Chief Black Hawk, Sauk

If the gentlemen of Virginia shall send us a dozen of their sons, we will take great care with their education, instruct them in all we know, and make men of them.

Chief Canassatego, Onondaga (at the Treaty of Lancaster)

*If women
could go into
your congress,
I think justice
would soon
be done to the
Indians.*

Sarah Winnemucca, Paiute

It was our belief that the love of possessions is a weakness to be overcome. Its appeal is to the material part, and if allowed its way, it will in time disturb one's spiritual balance. Therefore, children must early learn the beauty of generosity. They are taught to give what they prize most, that they may taste the happiness of giving.

Ohiyesa (Dr Charles Alexander Eastman),
Santee Dakota Sioux

He who would do great things should not attempt them all alone.

Seneca proverb

My young men shall never farm. Men who work the soil cannot dream, and wisdom comes to us in dreams.

Wovoka, Paiute

White men have too many chiefs.

Unknown Nez Percé

No river can return to its source, yet all rivers must have a beginning.

Unattributed proverb

We are all one child spinning through Mother Sky.

Shawnee proverb

A man or woman with many children has many homes.

Lakota Sioux proverb

We eat in silence, quietly smoke a pipe, and depart. Thus is our host honored. This is not the way of the white man. After his food has been eaten, one is expected to say foolish things. Then the host feels honored.

Chief Four Guns, Oglala Lakota Sioux

A people without a history is like the wind over buffalo grass.

Sioux proverb

All men were made by the same
Great Spirit Chief. They are all
brothers. The Earth is the mother
of all people, and all people should
have equal rights upon it.

Heinmot Tooyalaket (Chief Joseph), Nez Percé

Always give a word or sign of salute when meeting or passing a friend, or even a stranger, if in a lonely place. Show respect to all people, but grovel to none.

Chief Tecumseh, Shawnee

An Indian is an Indian regardless of the degree of Indian blood or which little government card they do or do not possess.

Chief Wilma Mankiller, Cherokee

It is easy, we think, to be loyal to family and clan, whose blood is in our own veins.

Ohiyesa (Dr Charles Alexander Eastman), Santee Dakota Sioux

And while I stood there I
saw more than I can tell,
And I understood more
than I saw;
For I was seeing in a
sacred manner the shapes
of things in the spirit,
And the shape of all
shapes as they must live
together like one being.

Black Elk, Oglala Lakota Sioux
(*from* Black Elk Speaks *by John G. Neihardt*)

Before our white brothers arrived to make us civilized men, we didn't have any kind of prison. Because of this, we had no delinquents. Without a prison, there can be no delinquents.
We had no locks nor keys and, therefore, among us there were no thieves.
When someone was so poor that he couldn't afford a horse, a tent or a blanket, he would, in that case, receive it all as a gift. We were too uncivilized to give great importance to private property. We didn't know any kind of money and consequently, the value of a human being was not determined by his wealth.
We had no written laws laid down, no lawyers, no politicians; therefore, we were not able to cheat and swindle one another.
We were really in bad shape before the white men arrived and I don't know how to explain how we were able to manage without these fundamental things that (so they tell us) are so necessary for a civilized society.

John Fire Lame Deer, Lakota Sioux

We have among us no exalted villains above the control of our laws. Daring wickedness here is never allowed to triumph over helpless innocence. The estates of widows and orphans are never devoured by enterprising swindlers.
We have no robbery under the pretext of law.

Thayendanegea (Joseph Brant), Mohawk

**The Indians in their simplicity
literally give away all that
they have—to relatives, to
guests of other tribes or clans,
but above all to the poor and
the aged, from whom they
can hope for no return.**

*Ohiyesa (Dr Charles Alexander Eastman),
Santee Dakota Sioux*

If we have corn and meat, and know of a family that has none, we divide with them. If we have more blankets than are sufficient, and others have not enough, we must give to them that want.

Chief Black Hawk, Sauk

Man's obsession with his own wants is taking him further from those without whom happiness cannot be found. It is taking him from his people.

From The Seven Paths: Changing One's Way of Walking in the World, *Anasazi Foundation*

Childbirth is best met alone, where no curious embarrass her, where all nature says to her spirit: It's love! It's love! The fulfilling of life!

Ohiyesa (Dr Charles Alexander Eastman), Santee Dakota Sioux

Not every sweet root gives birth to sweet grass.

Unattributed proverb

Remember that your children are not your own, but are lent to you by the Creator.

Mohawk proverb

I have seen that in any great undertaking it is not enough for a man to depend simply upon himself.

Isna-la-wica (Lone Man),
Lakota Sioux

One finger cannot lift a pebble.

Hopi proverb

You must teach your children that the ground beneath their feet is the ashes of our grandfathers. So that they will respect the land, tell your children that the earth is rich with the lives of our kin. Teach your children what we have taught our children, that the earth is our mother. Whatever befalls the earth befalls the sons of the earth. If men spit upon the ground they spit upon themselves.

Chief Seattle, Suqwamish and Duwamish

A man who would not love his father's grave is worse than a wild animal.

Heinmot Tooyalaket (Chief Joseph), Nez Percé

If you ever get married, my son, do not make an idol of your wife. The more you worship her, the more she will want to be worshiped.

Unknown Winnebago

Is it wrong for me to
love my own?
Is it wicked for me
because my skin is red?
Because I am Sioux?
Because I was born
where my father lived?
Because I would die
for my people and my
country?
God made me an Indian.

Tatanka Iyotanka (Sitting Bull), Hunkpapa
Lakota Sioux

Like the grasses showing tender faces to each other, thus should we do, for this was the wish of the Grandfathers of the World.

Black Elk, Oglala Lakota Sioux

No indiscretion can banish a woman from her parental lodge. It makes no difference how many children she may bring home; she is always welcome. The kettle is over the fire to feed them.

Chief Black Hawk, Sauk

Regard Heaven as your father, Earth as your Mother and all things as your Brothers and Sisters.

Unattributed proverb

Silence and isolation are the rule of life for the expectant mother. She wanders prayerful in the stillness of great woods, or on the bosom of the untrodden prairie, and to her poetic mind the imminent birth of her child prefigures the advent of a hero.

Ohiyesa (Dr Charles Alexander Eastman),
Santee Dakota Sioux

The traditions of our people are handed down from father to son. The Chief is considered to be the most learned, and the leader of the tribe. The Doctor, however, is thought to have more inspiration.

Sarah Winnemucca, Paiute

Try to do something for your people—something difficult. Have pity on your people and love them. If a man is poor, help him. Give him and his family food, give them whatever they ask for. If there is discord among your people, intercede. Take your sacred pipe and walk into their midst. Die if necessary in your attempt to bring about reconciliation. Then, when order has been restored and they see you lying dead on the ground, still holding in your hand the sacred pipe, the symbol of peace and reconciliation, then assuredly will they know that you have been a real chief.

Unknown Winnebago

Whether we have wings or fins, or roots or paws, we are all relatives.

Winona LaDuke, Ojibwe

With all things and in all things, we are relatives.

Sioux proverb

The success of my journey depended on whether my heart walked forward—toward my people—instead of backward, away from them.

From The Seven Paths: Changing One's Way of Walking in the World, *Anasazi Foundation*

I am truly astonished that the French have so little cleverness. They try to persuade us to convert our poles, our barks, and our wigwams into their houses of stone and of wood that are as tall and lofty as these trees. Very well! But why do men of five to six feet in height need houses that are sixty to eighty?

Micmac Chief (recorded by 17th-century French missionary Chrétien Le Clercq)

I have Indian blood in me. I have just enough white blood for you to question my honesty!

Will Rogers, Cherokee

Among the Indians there have been no written laws. Customs handed down from generation to generation have been the only laws to guide them. Every one might act different from what was considered right did he choose to do so, but such acts would bring upon him the censure of the Nation... This fear of the Nation's censure acted as a mighty band, binding all in one social, honorable compact.

Kahgegagahbowh (George Copway), Ojibwe

It is better to return a borrowed pot with a little something you last cooked in it.

Unattributed proverb

**No person among us
desires any other reward for
performing a brave and worthy
action, but the consciousness
of having served his nation.**

Thayendanegea (Joseph Brant), Mohawk

Our fathers gave us many laws, which they had learned from their fathers. These laws were good. They told us to treat all people as they treated us; that we should never be the first to break a bargain; that it was a disgrace to tell a lie; that we should only speak the truth; that it was a shame for one man to take from another his wife or his property without paying for it.

Heinmot Tooyalaket (Chief Joseph), Nez Percé

We are all poor because we are all honest.

Red Dog, Oglala Lakota Sioux

**Let us lead our children
To a good life and old age.
These our people; give
them good minds
To love one another.**

Mohawk prayer

Praise, flattery, exaggerated manners, and fine, high-sounding words were no part of Lakota politeness. Excessive manners were put down as insincere, and the constant talker was considered rude and thoughtless.

Chief Luther Standing Bear, Oglala Lakota Sioux

Love,
Peace, and
Happiness

The greatest strength is gentleness.

Iroquois proverb

I am poor and naked, but I am the chief of the nation. We do not want riches but we do want to train our children right. Riches would do us no good. We could not take them with us to the other world. We do not want riches. We want peace and love.

Chief Red Cloud, Oglala Lakota Sioux

I believe much trouble and blood would be saved if we opened our hearts more.

*Heinmot Tooyalaket (Chief Joseph),
Nez Percé*

I have learned that the point of life's walk is not where or how far I move my feet but how I am moved in my heart.

From The Seven Paths: Changing One's Way of Walking in the World, *Anasazi Foundation*

Can we talk of integration until there is integration of hearts and minds? Unless you have this, you only have a physical presence, and the walls between us are as high as the mountain range.

Geswanouth Slahoot (Chief Dan George),
Tsleil-Waututh Salish

If all would talk and then do as you have done, the sun of peace would shine forever.

Satank (Sitting Bear), Kiowa

It is not good enough to cry peace,
we must act peace, live peace, and
live in peace.

Shenandoah proverb

Our first teacher is our own heart.

Cheyenne proverb

Respect the gift and the giver.

Unattributed proverb

You must speak straight so that your words may go as sunlight into our hearts.

Chief Cochise (Like Ironweed), Chiricahua

If a man is as wise
as a serpent, he
can afford to be as
harmless as a dove.

Cheyenne proverb

Which of these is the wisest and happiest: he who labors without ceasing and only obtains, with great trouble, enough to live on, or he who rests in comfort and finds all that he needs in the pleasure of hunting and fishing?

Micmac Chief (recorded by 17th-century French missionary Chrétien Le Clercq)

Love yourself; get outside yourself and take action. Focus on the solution; be at peace.

Sioux proverb

The more you give, the more good things come to you.

Crow proverb

There is a road in the hearts of all of us, hidden and seldom traveled, which leads to an unknown, secret place.

Chief Luther Standing Bear,
Oglala Lakota Sioux

We are friends; we must assist each other to bear our burdens.

Osage proverb

A good chief gives, he does not take.

Mohawk proverb

A Nation is not conquered until the hearts of its women are on the ground. Then it is done, no matter how brave its warriors nor how strong its weapons.

Cheyenne proverb

Ask questions from your heart and you will be answered from the heart.

Omaha proverb

Certain things catch your eye, but pursue only those that capture your heart.

Unattributed proverb

Day and night cannot dwell together.

Duwamish proverb

Do not judge your neighbor until you walk two moons in his moccasins.

Cheyenne proverb

Do not wrong or hate your neighbor for it is not he that you wrong but yourself.

Pima proverb

Don't allow
the grass
to grow on
the path of
the friendship.

Unattributed proverb

Each bird loves to hear himself sing.

Arapaho proverb

Humor is the WD-40 of healing.

George Goodstriker, Kainai

The soul would have no rainbow if the eyes had no tears.

Unattributed proverb

If the Great Spirit had desired me to be a white man he would have made me so in the first place. He put in your heart certain wishes and plans, and in my heart he put other and different desires. It is not necessary for eagles to be crows.

Tatanka Iyotanka (Sitting Bull),
Hunkpapa Lakota Sioux

I see a time of Seven Generations when all the colors of mankind will gather under the Sacred Tree of Life and the whole Earth will become one circle again.

Tasunke Witko (Crazy Horse), Oglala Lakota Sioux

Inner peace and love are the greatest of God's gifts.

Lakota Sioux proverb

It does
not require
many words
to speak
the truth.

Heinmot Tooyalaket (Chief Joseph),
Nez Percé

Love between man and woman is founded on the mating instinct and is not free from desire and self-seeking. But to have a friend, and to be true under any and all trials, is the mark of a man!

Ohiyesa (Dr Charles Alexander Eastman), Santee Dakota Sioux

If you tie a horse to a stake, do you expect he will grow fat?

Heinmot Tooyalaket (Chief Joseph), Nez Percé

Force, no matter how concealed, begets resistance.

Lakota proverb

Love is something you and I must have. We must have it because our spirit feeds upon it. We must have it because without it we become weak and faint. Without love our self-esteem weakens. Without it our courage fails. Without love we can no longer look out confidently at the world. We turn inward and begin to feed upon our own personalities, and little by little we destroy ourselves. With it we are creative. With it we march tirelessly. With it, and with it alone, we are able to sacrifice for others.

Geswanouth Slahoot (Chief Dan George),
Tsleil-Waututh Salish

Love one another
and do not strive for
another's undoing.

Seneca proverb

Mother Earth
has never
been more
crowded, yet
her inhabitants
have never been
more lonely.

Anasazi Foundation

My heart is filled with joy when I see you here, as the brooks fill with water when the snows melt in the spring, and I feel glad, as the ponies are when the fresh grass starts in the beginning of the year.

Ten Bears, Yamparika Comanche

I heard of your coming, when I was many sleeps away, and I made but few camps before I met you. I knew that you had come to do good to me and to my people. I look for the benefits, which would last forever, and so my face shines with joy, as I look upon you.

Ten Bears, Yamparika Comanche

My heart laughs with joy because I am in your presence. Ah, how much more beautiful is the sun today than when you were angry with us!

Chitmachas Chief

Once I was in Victoria, and I saw a very large house. They told me it was a bank and that the white men place their money there to be taken care of, and that by and by they got it back with interest. We are Indians and we have no such bank, but when we have plenty of money or blankets, we give them away to other chiefs and people, and by and by they return them with interest, and our hearts feel good.
Our way of giving is our bank.

Chief Maquinna, Mowachaht

Out of the Indian approach to life there came a great freedom, an intense and absorbing respect for life, enriching faith in a Supreme Power, and principles of truth, honesty, generosity, equity, and brotherhood as a guide to mundane relations.

Black Elk, Oglala Lakota Sioux

One rain does not make a crop.

Creole proverb

Poverty is a noose that strangles humility and breeds disrespect for God and man.

Sioux proverb

Suppose a white man should come to me and say, Joseph, I like your horses. I want to buy them.

I say to him, no, my horses suit me; I will not sell them. Then he goes to my neighbor and he says, pay me money, and I will sell you Joseph's horses.

The white man returns to me and says, Joseph, I have bought your horses and you must let me have them.

If we sold our lands to the government, this is the way they bought them.

Heinmot Tooyalaket (Chief Joseph),
Nez Percé

The color of
skin makes no
difference. What is
good and just for
one is good and
just for the other,
and the Great
Spirit made all
men brothers.

Chief White Shield, Arikara

We always return to our first loves.

Unattributed proverb

My feet shall run because of you.
My feet dance because of you.
My eyes see because of you.
My mind thinks because of you.
And I shall love because of you.

Inuit wedding vow

We travel only as far and as high as our hearts will take us.

From The Seven Paths: Changing One's Way of Walking in the World, *Anasazi Foundation*

When a white army battles Indians and wins, it is called a great victory, but if they lose it is called a massacre.

Chief Cheeseekau, Shawnee

When the white man discovered this country Indians were running it. No taxes, no debt, women did all the work. White man thought he could improve on a system like this.

Cherokee proverb

Whether we walk among our people or alone among the hills, happiness in life's walking depends on how we feel about others in our hearts.

From The Seven Paths: Changing One's Way of Walking in the World, *Anasazi Foundation*

Women should never
be watched too closely.
If you try to watch
them, you will merely
show your jealousy and
become so jealous of
your wife that she will
leave you and run away.
You yourself will be to
blame for this.

Unknown Winnebago

Would it surprise you to hear that man's unhappiness is due in large measure to the way he is seeking after happiness?

From The Seven Paths: Changing One's Way of Walking in the World, *Anasazi Foundation*

Each man is good in the sight of the Great Spirit.

Chief Sitting Bull, Hunkpapa Lakota Sioux

A long time ago
this land belonged
to our fathers,
but when I go up
to the river I see
camps of soldiers
on its banks. These
soldiers cut down
my timber, they kill
my buffalo and when
I see that, my heart
feels like bursting.

Chief Satanta, Kiowa

Great Spirit, I want no blood upon my land to stain the grass. I want it clear and pure, and I wish it so, that all who go through among my people may find it peaceful when they come, and leave peacefully when they go.

Chief Ten Bears, Yamparika Comanche

No nation, I think,
can be more
fond of novelties
than the English;
they gaze upon
foreigners as
if they had just
dropped down
from the moon.

*Kahkewaquonaby (Sacred Waving
Feathers, later Peter Jones), Ojibwe*

The white man says there is freedom and justice for all. We have had freedom and justice, and that is why we have been almost exterminated. We shall not forget this.

Chief Tecumseh, Shawnee

The first peace, which is the most important, is that which comes within the souls of people when they realize their relationship, their oneness, with the universe and all its powers, and when they realize that at the center of the universe dwells Wakan-Taka (the Great Spirit), and that this center is really everywhere, it is within each of us. This is the real peace, and the others are but reflections of this.

Black Elk, Oglala Lakota Sioux

The second peace is that which is made between two individuals, and the third is that which is made between two nations.

Black Elk, Oglala Lakota Sioux

But above all you should
understand that there can never be
peace between nations until there
is known that true peace, which,
as I have often said, is within the
souls of men.

Black Elk, Oglala Lakota Sioux

We gave them forest-clad mountains and valleys full of game, and in return what did they give our warriors and our women? Rum, trinkets, and a grave.

Chief Tecumseh, Shawnee

When you hunt for rattlesnake, you usually cannot find it —and perhaps it will bite you before you see it.

Chief Shingis, Delaware

Why should you take by force from us that which you can obtain by love? Why should you destroy us who have provided you with food? What can you get by war?

King Wahunsonacook, Powhatan

I asked for a person to love that I might never be alone; I was given a life of a hermit, that I might learn to accept myself.

Olympic gold medalist Billy Mills, Oglala Lakota Sioux

319

*Prayers,
Blessings,
and the
Great
Spirit*

*Give me knowledge,
so I may have
kindness for all.*

Unattributed prayer

*Everything the power of the world
does is done in a circle.
The sky is round and I have heard that
the earth is round like a ball
and so are all the stars. The wind, in
its greatest power, whirls.
Birds make their nests in circles, for
theirs is the same religion as ours.*

Black Elk, Oglala Lakota Sioux

If the Great and the Good Spirit wished us to believe and do as the whites, he could easily change our opinions, so that we would see, and think, and act as they do. We are nothing compared to His power, and feel and know it.

Chief Black Hawk, Sauk

Let me be a free man, free to travel,
free to stop, free to work, free to trade
where I choose, free to choose my own
teachers, free to follow the religion of
my fathers, free to think and talk and
act for myself, and I will obey every law,
or submit to the penalty.

Heinmot Tooyalaket (Chief Joseph), Nez Percé

Oh, God in Heaven!
Give me back the
courage of the olden
Chiefs. Let me wrestle
with my surroundings.
Let me again, as in the
days of old, dominate
my environment. Let
me humbly accept
this new culture and
through it rise up and
go on.

Geswanouth Slahoot (Chief Dan George),
Tsleil-Waututh Salish

Let me walk in beauty and make my eyes ever behold the red and purple sunset. Make my hands respect the things you have made and my ears sharp to hear your voice.

Great Spirit Prayer, translated by Chief Yellow Lark, Lakota Sioux

Every man's religion is good. There is none of it bad. We are all trying to arrive at the same place according to our own conscience and teachings. It don't matter which road you take.

Will Rogers, Cherokee

Everyone makes his feast as he thinks best, to please the Great Spirit, who has the care of all beings created.

Chief Black Hawk, Sauk

Each soul must meet the morning sun, the new, sweet earth, and the Great Silence alone!

Ohiyesa (Dr Charles Alexander Eastman), Santee Dakota Sioux

*Earth teach me quiet—as the grasses
are still with new light.
Earth teach me suffering—as old
stones suffer with memory.
Earth teach me humility—as blossoms
are humble with beginning.
Earth teach me caring—as mothers
nurture their young.
Earth teach me courage—as the tree
that stands alone.
Earth teach me limitation—as the ant
that crawls on the ground.
Earth teach me freedom—as the eagle
that soars in the sky.
Earth teach me acceptance—as the
leaves that die each fall.
Earth teach me renewal—as the seed
that rises in the spring.
Earth teach me to forget myself—as
melted snow forgets its life.
Earth teach me to remember kindness
—as dry fields weep with rain.*

Ute prayer

Give thanks for unknown blessings already on their way.

Unattributed proverb

I am going to venture that the man who sat on the ground in his tipi meditating on life and its meaning, accepting the kinship of all creatures, and acknowledging unity with the universe of things, was infusing into his being the true essence of civilization.

Chief Luther Standing Bear,
Oglala Lakota Sioux

I am the Spirit's janitor... all I do is wipe the windows a bit, so you can see out for yourself.

Godfrey Chips, Oglala Lakota Sioux

I salute the light within your eyes where the whole Universe dwells. For when you are at that center within you and I am in that place within me, we shall be one.

Tasunke Witko (Crazy Horse), Oglala Lakota Sioux

*May the stars carry
your sadness away,
May the flowers fill
your heart with beauty,
May hope forever wipe
away your tears.
And above all, may
silence make you
strong.*

*Geswanouth Slahoot (Chief Dan George),
Tsleil-Waututh Salish*

Oh, Great Spirit,
Help me always to speak the truth quietly,
To listen with an open mind when others speak,
And to remember the peace that may be found in silence.

Cherokee prayer

Religion is for people who are afraid of going to hell. Spirituality is for those who have already been there.

Vine Deloria Jr., Oglala Lakota Sioux

Sometimes I go about pitying myself, and all the while I am being carried across the sky by beautiful clouds.

Ojibwe proverb

The First Nations shall rise again and it shall be a blessing for a sick world; a world filled with broken promises, selfishness, and separations; a world longing for light again.

Tasunke Witko (Crazy Horse),
Oglala Lakota Sioux

Trouble no one about his religion. Respect others in their views and demand that they respect yours.

Chief Tecumseh, Shawnee

Upon this earth, on which we live, Unseen has power.
This power is mine, for locating the enemy.
I search for that enemy, which only Unseen the Great can show to me.

Lozen, Chihenne Chiricahua Apache

Wakan Tanka, Great Mystery, teach me
how to trust my heart, my mind, my
intuition, my inner knowing, the senses
of my body, the blessings of my spirit.
Teach me to trust these things so that
I may enter my Sacred Space and
love beyond my fear, and thus walk
in balance with the passing of each
glorious Sun.

Lakota Sioux prayer

We return thanks to our mother, the Earth, which sustains us.
We return thanks to the rivers and streams, which supply us with water.
We return thanks to all herbs, which furnish medicines for the cure of our diseases.
We return thanks to the moon and stars, which have given to us their light when the sun was gone.
We return thanks to the sun, that has looked upon the earth with a beneficent eye.
Lastly, we return thanks to the Great Spirit, in Whom is embodied all goodness, and Who directs all things for the good of Her children.

Iroquois prayer

When you are in doubt,
be still, and wait.
When doubt no longer
exists for you, then go
forward with courage.
So long as mists
envelop you, be still.
Be still until the
sunlight pours through
and dispels the mists,
as it surely will.
Then act with courage.

Chief White Eagle, Ponca

When you rise in the morning, give thanks for the light, for your life, for your strength. Give thanks for your food and for the joy of living.
If you see no reason to give thanks, the fault lies in yourself.

Chief Tecumseh, Shawnee

Whenever, in the course of the daily hunt, the hunter comes upon a scene that is strikingly beautiful, or sublime—a black thundercloud with the rainbow's glowing arch above the mountain, a white waterfall in the heart of a green gorge, a vast prairie tinged with the blood-red of the sunset—he pauses for an instant in the attitude of worship. He sees no need for a setting apart one day in seven as a holy day, because to him all days are God's days.

Ohiyesa (Dr Charles Alexander Eastman), Santee Dakota Sioux

347

A hungry stomach makes a short prayer.

Paiute proverb

Everything the power does, it does in a circle.

Lakota proverb

God gives us
each a song.

Ute proverb

**I cannot think
that we are
useless or God
would not have
created us.**

Geronimo, Apache

Sharing and giving are the ways of God.

Sauk proverb

A real comfort is better than an artificial one to the human nature.

Maungwudaus (George Henry), Ojibwe

The rainbow is a sign from Him who is in all things.

Hopi proverb

There are no political solutions to spiritual problems.

Unknown Chief

All things in the world are
two. In our minds we are
two, good and evil. With
our eyes we see two things,
things that are fair and things
that are ugly.
We have the right hand that
strikes and makes for evil,
and we have the left hand full
of kindness, near the heart.
One foot may lead us to an
evil way, the other foot may
lead us to a good.
So are all things two, all two.

Letakos-Lesa (Eagle Chief), Pawnee

If there is but one religion, why do you white people differ so much about it?

Sogoyewapha (Red Jacket), Seneca

Brother! We are told that you have been preaching to the white people in this place... We will wait a little while, and see what effect your preaching has upon them. If we find it does them good and makes them honest and less disposed to cheat us, we will then consider again becoming Christians.

Sogoyewapha (Red Jacket), Seneca

For after all the great religions have
been preached and expounded,
or have been revealed by brilliant
scholars, or have been written in
fine books and embellished in fine
language with finer covers, man—
all man—is still confronted by the
Great Mystery.

Chief Luther Standing Bear,
Oglala Lakota Sioux

There is one
God looking
down on us all.
We are all the
children of one
God. The sun,
the darkness,
the winds are
all listening to
what we have
to say.

Geronimo, Apache

I was standing on the highest mountain of them all, and round about beneath me was the whole hoop of the world. And while I stood there I saw more than I can tell and I understood more than I saw; for I was seeing in a sacred manner the shapes of all things in the spirit, and the shape of all shapes as they must live together like one being.

Black Elk, Oglala Lakota Sioux

In the beginning of all things, wisdom and knowledge were with the animals, for Tirawa, the One Above, did not speak directly to man. He sent certain animals to tell men that he showed himself through the beast, and that from them, and from the stars and the sun and moon should man learn. All things tell of Tirawa.

Letakos-Lesa (Eagle Chief), Pawnee

The Indian needs no writings; words that are true sink deep into his heart, where they remain. He never forgets them.

Four Guns, Oglala Lakota Sioux

And I saw that the
sacred hoop of my
people was one of many
hoops that made one
circle, wide as daylight
and as starlight, and
in the center grew one
mighty flowering tree
to shelter all children of
one mother and
one father.
And I saw that it
was holy.

Black Elk, Oglala Lakota Sioux

This is a holy song, and great is its power. The song tells how, as I sing, I go through the air to a holy place where Yusun (The Supreme Being) will give me power to do wonderful things. I am surrounded by little clouds, and as I go through the air I change, becoming spirit only.

Geronimo, Apache

When a man does a piece of work which is admired by all, we say that it is wonderful; but when we see the changes of day and night, the sun, the moon, and the stars in the sky, and the changing seasons upon the earth, with their ripening fruits, anyone must realize that it is the work of someone more powerful than man.

Chief Luther Standing Bear, Oglala Lakota Sioux

We walk in our moccasins upon the Earth
And beneath the sky
As we travel on life's path of beauty
We will live a good life and reach old age.

Navajo blessing

Oh Great Spirit, bring to our brothers
the wisdom of Nature
And the knowledge that if her laws
are obeyed
This land will again flourish and
grasses and trees will grow as before.

*Jasper Saunkeah, Cherokee (from the Native
Commandments)*

Let us not listen to the voices of the two-hearted, the destroyers of mind, the haters and self-made leaders, whose lusts for power and wealth will lead us into confusion and darkness. Seek visions always of world beauty, not violence nor battlefields.

Hopi prayer

Guide those that, through their councils, seek to spread the wisdom of their leaders to all people. Heal the raw wounds of the earth and restore to our soul the richness which strengthens men's bodies and makes them wise in their councils.

*Jasper Saunkeah,
Cherokee (from the Native
Commandments)*

Oh, Great Spirit,
Help me to remain calm and
strong in the face of all that
comes toward me.
Let me learn the lessons
you have hidden in every
leaf and rock.
Help me seek pure thoughts
and act with the intention of
helping others.
Help me find compassion
without empathy
overwhelming me.

Great Spirit Prayer

369

Bring to all the knowledge that great cities live only through the bounty of the good earth beyond their paved streets and towers of stone and steel.

Jasper Saunkeah, Cherokee (from the Native Commandments)

All over the earth the faces
of living things are all alike.
With tenderness have these
come up out of the ground.
Look upon these faces of
children without number and
with children in their arms
That they may face the
winds and walk the good
road to the day of quiet.
This is my prayer, hear me!

Black Elk, Oglala Lakota Sioux

May the Warm Winds of Heaven
blow softly upon your house.
May the Great Spirit bless all who
enter there.
May your mocassins make happy
tracks in many snows.
And may the rainbow always
touch your shoulder.

Sioux Prayer, translated by Lakota Sioux Chief
Yellow Lark

I make my prayer for all people, the children, the women, and the men. I pray that no harm will come to them, and that on the great island, there be no war, that there be no ill feelings among us.
From this day on may we walk hand in hand.
So be it.

Frank Fools Crow, Oglala Lakota Sioux (from his prayer before the U.S. Senate in 1975)

If a man is to do something more than human, he must have more than human powers.

Unattributed proverb

Now you will feel no rain, for each of you will be shelter to the other.
Now you will feel no cold, for each of you will be warmth to the other.
Now there is no more loneliness, for each of you will be companion to the other.
Now you are two bodies, but there is one life before you.
Go now to your dwelling place, to enter into the days of your togetherness. And may your days be good and long upon the earth.

Apache wedding blessing

God in heaven above, please protect the ones
we love.
We honor all you created as we pledge our
hearts and lives together.
We honor Mother Earth and ask for our
marriage to be abundant and grow stronger
through the seasons.
We honor fire and ask that our union be warm
and glowing with love in our hearts.
We honor wind and ask we sail through life
safe and calm as in our father's arms.
We honor water to clean and soothe our
relationship, that it may never thirst for love.
With all the forces of the universe you created,
we pray for harmony and true happiness as
we forever grow young together.

Cherokee wedding prayer

Sky our grandfather
Moon our grandmother
Earth our Mother
I am thankful
We love each other
We are grateful.

Cherokee prayer

O our Father, the Sky,
hear us and make us
strong.
O our Mother, the Earth,
hear us and give us
support.
O Spirit of the East, send
us your Wisdom.
O Spirit of the South,
may we tread your path.
O Spirit of the West, may
we always be ready for
the long journey.
O Spirit of the North,
purify us with your
cleansing winds.

Sioux prayer

Great Spirit of Light, come to me out of the East with the power of the rising sun. Let there be light in my words, let there be light on my path that I walk. Let me remember always that you give the gift of a new day. And never let me be burdened with sorrow by not starting over again.

Prayer to the Four Directions,
Chief Seattle, Suqwamish
and Duwamish

Great Spirit of Love, come
to me with the power
of the North. Make me
courageous when the cold
wind falls upon me. Give
me strength and endurance
for everything that is harsh,
everything that hurts,
everything that makes me
squint. Let me move through
life ready to take what comes
from the north.

Prayer to the Four Directions, Chief Seattle,
Suqwamish and Duwamish

Great Life-Giving Spirit,
I face the West, the
direction of sundown.
Let me remember every
day that the moment will
come when my sun will go
down. Never let me forget
that I must fade into you.
Give me a beautiful color,
give me a great sky for
setting, so that when it is
my time to meet you, I can
come with glory.

Prayer to the Four Directions, Chief Seattle,
Suqwamish and Duwamish

Great Spirit of Creation, send me the warm and soothing winds from the South. Comfort me and caress me when I am tired and cold. Unfold me like the gentle breezes that unfold the leaves on the trees. As you give to all the earth your warm, moving wind, give to me, so that I may grow close to you in warmth.

Prayer to the Four Directions, Chief Seattle, Suqwamish and Duwamish

Make me wise so that I may understand the things you have taught my people.
Let me learn the lessons you have hidden in every leaf and rock.
I seek strength, not to be greater than my brother, but to fight my greatest enemy—myself.

Great Spirit Prayer, translated by Chief Yellow Lark, Lakota Sioux